MATADORA

MATADORA

Sarah Gambito

ALICE JAMES BOOKS
FARMINGTON, MAINE

10 9 8 7 6 5 4 3 2 1

Alice James Books are published by Alice James Poetry
Cooperative, Inc., an affiliate of the University of
Maine at Farmington.

Alice James Books
238 Main Street
Farmington, ME 04938

www.alicejamesbooks.org

Library of Congress Cataloging-in-Publication Data
Gambito, Sarah Verdes.
  Matadora / Sarah Gambito.
    p. cm.
  ISBN 1-882295-48-X
  1. Filipino American women--Poetry. 2. Feminist poetry, American. 3. Sex
role--Poetry. 4. Women--Poetry. I. Title.
  PS3607.A433M38 2004
  811'.6--dc22
                            2004015621

Alice James Book gratefully acknowledges support from
the University of Maine at Farmington and the National
Endowment for the Arts. ❦

Cover art by Edward del Rosario

Again, for my Family

"To become the Topaz Bird somehow," I said, pausing for a moment
trying to picture this. "It has the most magnificent—"
"Plumage," my mother said. I loved the way she said plumage,
the beautiful mouth she made for the word plumage.
"Plumage," I said, trying to imitate her.

— CAROLE MASO

CONTENTS

Acknowledgements

Grateful acknowledgement is made to the following publications, where these poems first appeared:

The Antioch Review: "The Glitter Lamb"
Brooklyn Review: "Blackberrying"
Black Warrior Review: "Untitled"
Fence: "Fear," "How to Make Your Daughter an American (Again)"
Interlope: "Paloma Loves," "The Daily Bride"
The Iowa Review: "My Parting Gift Story," "Scene: A Loom"
The New Republic: "Dear Elation, There Is Somthing Else You Didn't Know"
Quarterly West: "Paloma's Church in America"

My deep gratitude goes out to the following people and organizations who helped me bring this book alive.

My Family, especially my sister, Christine Rodgers, Pavneet Singh, Joseph O. Legaspi, Charlotte Meehan, Eddie del Rosario, Kron Vollmer, Mita Ghosal, The FireCircle Collective, Marie Sarmiento, Priya Yadav, Jimmy Yan, Mei-mei Berssenbrugge, Matt Paco, Sue Mi Ko, Emily Dalton, Marilyn Rifkin, Woodie Rea, Forrest Gander, Charles Wright, Rita Dove, Keith & Rosmarie Waldrop, Aishah Rahman, Amy Dudley, Tony Paterno, Diane Fincher, Ms. Perry, Keri Claiborne, Connie Yuan, Blossom, The Creative Writing Program at Brown University, The Millay Colony for the Arts, Café Orlin

Veronicas

These passes were designed to show the matador's skill and art with the cape, his domination of the bull and also to fix the bull in a certain spot before the entry of the horses. They are called veronicas after St. Veronica who wiped the face of Our Lord with a cloth....

—ERNEST HEMINGWAY
Death in the Afternoon

Gayon na lamang ang pag-ibig ng Diyos sa sanlibutan, kaya ibinigay niya ang kanyang bugtong na Anak, upang ang sumampalataya sa kanya ay hindi mapahamak, kundi magkaroon ng buhay na walang hanggan.

Gayon na *God knew* g-ibig ng Diyos sa sanlibutan, kaya ibinigay niya ang kanyang bugtong na *another language* lataya sa kanya ay hindi mapahamak, kundi magkaroon ng buhay na walang hanggan.

Gayon na lamang ang pag-ibig ng Diyos sa sanlibutan, kaya ibinigay niya ang kanyang bugtong na Anak, upang ang *pretty well.* a sa kanya ay hindi mapahamak, kundi magkaroon ng buhay na walang hanggan.

Gayon *In another language, he drank Pelligrino water.* ya ibinigay niya ang kanyang bugtong na Anak, upang ang sumampalataya sa kanya ay hindi mapahamak, kundi *He left gift-bags for comrades.* ggan.

Gayon na *He drew reindeer.* ng Diyos sa sanlibutan, kaya ibinigay niya ang kanyang bugtong na Anak, upang ang sumampalataya sa kanya ay hindi mapahamak, kundi magkaroon ng buhay na walang hanggan.

Gayon na *Paloma would have written about this but she does not write every day in her Light Journal. Paloma buys jewelry.* g buhay na walang hanggan.

Gayon *I noticed a new garnet in her ear the other day. But she* ay niya ang kanyang bugtong na Anak, upang ang sumampalataya sa kanya ay hindi mapahamak, kundi magkaroon *wanted me to notice her scarf.*

Gayon na lamang *She pointed to it and said,* libutan, kaya ibinigay niya ang kanyang bugtong na Anak, up *Now, I am Paloma of the Mountains* ak, kundi magkaroon ng buhay na walang hanggan.

FAMILY DAY

Whereas the US has spent decades bemoaning the export of its jobs (to Mexico, to China), the Philippine government revels in the export of its people. 100 million cell phone messages a day are why overseas Filipino workers and their families remain families....

—*Wired*, June 2002

I'm sand surfing. Waiting for a bad boy to come home.

About ten percent of the skilled population read anyone

who knows how to do anything is hard

at work outside the country.

I am fourteen waiting for the next freedom.

What's crazy is I'm homesick for him.

Handpicked teachers, who are given crash courses

in Georgia history or California politics

before they arrive on US soil.

I want him to come home so I can wrap

my five-dollar arms around him.

What sets the Philippines apart is that the federal government

avidly encourages the flow.

Countries like ours, rich in human resources,

have that to contribute to the rest of the world.

Embrace our role as temp agency to the world.

I do the laundry. I know the residents. Yet, where is he.

I have a niece in Italy, a nephew in Bern,

another nephew in Brussels.

I have nieces in Los Angeles and New Jersey.

How when he was showing me around London.

How I felt so special.

Please come home as I am lovesick.

"Look Asian, think Spanish, act American."

I never thought I'd be here waiting for a valentine.

Each 160-character message costs one peso (two US cents).

There was this one, a matadora, one for whom my trap shuts sharp. Surely, even now, she is blackberrying trying to prove me wrong. She says, "Oh, I am only a trickling of looking good." All this while her mouth is stained. And she relishes. She moves with more caring.

My corazon said put a lid on it for God's sakes, put a lid on it. But she doesn't and I die of gratitude. She can be anyone. In fact, she prefers me moving.

Once, she was at a funeral. I overheard her arguing politely with a lover. He had brought food to another woman. This was her appetite—he was saying—these were her roses of surprise. My matadora said, "This is not the time." But, she watched the woman eat and it was a more tender sight. I think he is still standing by those graves.

Don't forget the other Americas.
A garden of cooling deer.
Vehicle toward nightly and lambent end.

I am only these words for you.
America loves americans.
America loves the ocean between the World Wars.
Wouldn't you know me?

I inhabit the millions
shielded, shellacked and holding
the plush soul of the immigrant's soul in America.

Who in this house will admit to my amethyst ring?
If you are here, I feel you almost recognize me.

I fall bemused with a painter.
Painting apricots and no-nonsense.
Make mistakes faster.
Said my racehorse. Said my Make It Clang.

SCENE: A LOOM

If I emulate you, where would my rafters be?
She pulls out her voice scale by scale.
She thinks I do not hear her emotion.
This is a shock.

To make it more specific—*my people.*

Children are the imminent sojourn.
A maybe of love.
Brilliant persuasion from the stands.

I buy you a plate of expensive pears.
I cut the pear in ½.

January 8th	We eat a ½.
January 8th	Someone dear to me has died.
	Someone dear to me has died.
January 28th	Ito ay isang pagdasal para sa kapatid ko, meaning

He was unkind and she loved him.
He left her on the impended highway and she loved him.
He went away to the far country and she loved him.

I do not know the Lord.
But he spoke in a lovely way.
Created. Silvery citadel.

Across the street a beautiful asian was burning. I took my sandals off. Seven times hotter the fire remembered babies. And canals of babies burning it back. I took off your sandals, and your sandals, too. Sometimes we waited for stone tablets. Most often we brewed what tea we could of the desert. Silicate, mica, a mysterious formica. We drank and became practiced. We missed our mothers. Our mothers couldn't call. We called in dreams. We dreamed illnesses on our new bodies. The bodies clung to covenants. The covenants, in turn, drove to scholarship. (Stewardship, pharmacists like to say. Star Connection, my Tanenbaum makes to say.) So many babies, the asian said. Across the street a beautiful iconoclast was burning. I do remember that dream more than all—that I did not doubt. Your Honor, I saw the future.

FEAR

A girl as a gem. I saw the worthiness of the gem.

But I was not the gem and I was not the jeweler.

One thousand people gather for the resurrection.

Their duty to the commonplace.

She's waving as if she might lose. She is your sister.

A corona. A beggar of lilies.

A platform for the operetta to begin.

Bring in the butcher and his life in service.

THE WOMEN OF TAGAYTAY GATHER AT THE EDGE OF THE LUSTROUS RIVER AND SEE THE SPIRIT OF GOD IN A WHITE BIRD

Girlfriend didn't see shit.

Girlfriend found out
the need of God
is God.

God: I was walking down the street when I found you.

His Absence: One little, two little, three little.

God: And I was positioning the tableau. Like so. This and this. Further near the scapular.

His Absence: And did you know the sister waited. All long the dead dry shore. And for fourteen weathers. We did not kick any one of them. Not you. Not the cloud over the house. Did you know that house. Fourteen black clopping creatures made known to me.

God: Me.

His Absence: Four photographs: one—candyapple, two—a swan drinking, three and four, a ship coming to shore. La o la eh. Down by the river by the sinking sea. There were four of them and: verbose, vanished, verde grande. I inform you, I beseech you, O Capulet, you of little faith.

God: Grounded. In the house, four sisters. Steel downtown. One: marriage at eighteen years old. Two: skidding down Fifth Ave. Three and four: oh dolly.

His Absence: Fifth Ave is where you met them. Admit. Admit.

God: Who are the three crestfallen angels?

His Absence: There was a certain man who did not believe in
                numbers. This man had a donkey.

God: And the donkey did not talk.

His Absence: The donkey said: I waited for you by the
                crestfallen sea.

God: FIVE GOOD THOUGHTS FOR OUR DELIGHTED ONE.
                WHO WAITED ALL THE CRESTFALLEN NIGHT.

His Absence: Grounded: September in Manhattan. You did
                not open the can of peas. You did not see me
                reading over the books. I was kissing for you.

God: I kissed the elevator.

His Absence: I'm kissing you now.

God: You fail me.

His Absence: Listen to me.

(Silence)

God: Me.

His Absence: Caveat: The dolly in the mirror. It is important
                that he understands *himself. His* vulnerability
                and mine. His journals in Russia. My four sisters.
                His best friend who had died. My sister's birth
                control. It is related to you. They know as they
                drive in his car. The car has California license
                plates.

God: Something in transit is in love.

His Absence:	You are entrusted by yourself to the possibilities of yourself.
God:	By post: naturally. Expect it in three days.
His Absence:	Not enough time.
God:	I expect you here. And I expect you on time.
His Absence:	I arose from the canopy of a man to a tinning sound.

(Silence)

His Absence:	I am. Of interest to you.

(Silence)

God:	*(making a gun with his fingers)* If I aim....

(Silence)

His Absence:	*(making a gun with his fingers and leveling it at God)* If I aim....
God:	If I aim, move.

I believed we could say me bead by bead.
That we sat in our assembly.
Head bowed, trees overcast.

He's a freakaphone. The type of guy who enjoys reading about
the fabulous comfort women. There is the idea that she might say,
"Your life is in danger. You must leave."

244 E. 17th Street, New York, NY 10003

To say this is the spot.

That I am not a lighthouse, a brinkhouse.
I mean I rent her
I shoulder her despite my sister.

I enjoy women, but I love you.
I smell cherries when I think of love.
I seem so hopeful and full of vacations.
My smallest and sleeping self blowsing around
the students of clarinets.

GRIEF GOD

You look and soon these two worlds
Leave you.

I already know that I leap out.
That absolutely alone.
I am such a long way in.

Gripping the endless and ground-shaking book of prayer.

Your details are my best strength
As curling birds climb into the witch of heaven.

I lie flat.

My possessions resemble efforts

I who feel close to you, my family.
Our house is like enormous riches.

It heals others, it makes me sick.
But I'm like a sick king, composed.

My feathers are marvelous.
I deceive you.
I still hold through the doors of the tomb trays.
I want to hold it.

Suerte de Recibir

Suerte de Recibir is to kill the bull from in front awaiting his charge with the sword without moving. Letting the bull come until man and bull become one figure as the sword goes in. Most difficult, dangerous and emotional way to kill bulls....

—ERNEST HEMINGWAY
Death in the Afternoon

At the mere hint of doubt, he would push aside his plate and say:
"This meal has been prepared without love."

—GABRIEL GARCIA MARQUEZ
Love in the Time of Cholera

I

How I wanted to see us: naiad and nathan
and proud for somebody.

Here's another story:

II

We found an elegant girl.
Some say she was a cornfield.
I say she was a sword in a cornfield.
The swordsmen say she was a girl and the sword did not save her.

What are the endings that bring in the bacon?
How I want to work for them.

"Hello special."

I won't tell you that.
(sotto voce) I won't tell you that.

"Give me the name of an actress you hate," you said.

III

I'll show you that she never gave you up.

I am a lamp.

I'll be wrong sometimes.

So, do I once again make it easy for you.

Someone is already showing three scratches on a young arm.
Light glamours from beneath. Utility.

For example:

A woman goes into a department store with two rabbit-eared
children. She's worked the nine-hour shift and still has managed
to make it to choir rehearsal (though she lip-synched). The
children haven't seen her all day and are excited to show off. They
blend in with the clothes. Wool, acetate, rayon and fake fur!
Where are they now? She feels like crying.

I can think of _____ theoretically.

People without secure attachment figures may first seek _____ in a partner. Once they master this, they seek out a partner similar to their absent childhood authority figure and try to make the person _____ them.

"making them tick"

Not groin-teasing hula dances
strange web-sites

My sweet scent.

Talked to _____ last night as I should have not.

I have a dream.
I am playing a board game with acquaintances.
I must choose from:

1. Man
2. Men
3. My Heart

What my heart said:

I'm sexually _____ our children. I'm plotting to _____ you very soon.

We go to clubs. We go to restaurants. We go to cafes. We go to raw bars. An acquaintance fashions a representative sculpture. I felt her face consumed by the veil, its raining, deeper points.

She was steps to dancing.

I was dancing so much that I thought that way.

Given the irascibility of watercolor—how it assumes the inexactitude of commodities like frustration and woman at window, it cannot be surprising that beneath every canvas there is a pond that is, in a word, swift.

There is a street in Tagaytay. Villagers lift their children on their shoulders. The children clap their hands. The sound of clapping echoes through the street in Tagaytay. Echoes through the porcelain cup she holds standing by the window.

If there is time for deliberation, then there will be time for epiphany. Grains of sand clattering on the floor. Fluttering movement—a hand reaching for a hot supper, a lucid wind chime. There is a black livingroom—figures in silhouette. What they do not say is written in a red book where a violinist simultaneously composes intermezzos made of grass, of cyclical action.

Going to the movies alone. Saying to the ticket-lady, "one please..." is a catharsis that is a gold leaf. Beating of the drum bleeds for the rarest time. It occurred to him that her braid was his only friendship. A man walking down a crowded street. He's looking into headlights that close his eyes, prepare him for walking down a crowded street.

She is sitting in her mother's house. Blare worthy enough to swim in. Once I have a sister. I stand at the door but cannot knock. I think I am a failure. My sister marries. I hold her flowers while she walks sedately into the unfurling ocean. My little lamb. My baby haze.

Sometimes I remember the lanterns my grandmother made. Paper alight, awing. They say more than you ever did. Bobbing in the night.

Once my father was trying to speak and I did not listen. My eyes were lowered and maybe that would have been enough. But he fell silent. Raked his fingers through his hair. This was how he missed me.

Her husband gave her the green shell. See this shell. She filled it with the meekest flower she could find. But he could smell her heart. Pieces of sand, bits of a necklace I wore as a child.

Outside, the men are burning sugar cane. It is the movement of a crane taking flight. The water jiggles with longing, circles of departure. No one can look at the rainbow.

I can't stand the dark. Vampires come out. They lunge at me. They are both male and female. They have wings on their shoulders. They are smug in their lazy flights in my room. They wear designer clothes. They copulate in front of me.

She is trying to run but she is lying down and she is dead. Her face is a skull and a face. The candle gutters and can never go out.

She was six when she saw her first rainbow. She was riding her bike in jerky circles to avoid the puddles. Her father said, "Look, a rainbow." She looked up and so it was.

Hope is Longer than Time

Over here my pretty little sow cow.
Over the noise, a house gathers together.

In her mind, vapors of a planned stairwell.
All sorts of people bubbly and giving thanks.

In the chamber of chambers, a pair of wings
is fitted with a construct.

That I grab you by your muscles.
And that the bed reasserts itself.

Five years ago, we might have believed
the credits flying upwards.

But I plunked you down
semi-circles and alto.

Closer there is an especial filigree.
The names of ancestral angels are written thereon.

The syllables coming down
like supposed rain. One—one thousand, two—one thousand.

Longer to stay outdoors, to count by blade
the how many times we did not live.

Eating is a miracle unto itself.
What flies past has grown older.

It knows its words, its stepping responsibility.
I spread you out. Low over months.

One—one thousand, two—one thousand, three—one thousand.
Up close it's my friends going by.

New York (Radio Edit)

I was already wearing our daughter's bracelet.

(This is a coral only it became too connected to other people.)

I needed it to last through many wearing and sleeping
and watching and soaping.

Scene: We walked through the museum and he scoffed the
         whole live-long way.

                    My keyhole: Go yourself. See for yourself.

We mistake the sharky emotion.
The one to speak up last.

I leave the argument behind to caprice along
with my impatient seal-stealing body.

I do all that I want.

Feeling it is what leaked out from the fighter's hands.

I (Asian girl) was eating pasta with a dancer (Asian girl) last night
in front of the Asian-American tirade. She quoted a book of
144,000 blank pages and she said, sometimes do you feel crazy? I
was biting off my chicken. I said let's go through an exercise.

Someone is sleeping very peacefully in a bed next to you.
Who is this person?

A sculptor (from LA he said just visiting) listened to us. He said
I'm working on a 50-foot bamboo thing. He said you should
come by.

And we are still in our twenties.
Her. With her jute little girl bag.
Me in bathroom in London with roommates with little hope.

A bear of a relationship.
The man because his voice was a malediction
and the woman and her three fairhair brady kids.
How they ** on the hotel bed. And that they needed each other.

Who puts up with all that flack.
While I spine in my la France university aquarium.
Contort. Swipe. Play.

She a cyclamen he, he a cyclamen.
I was often proud of them as some other Africas.
Reappareled and licking their hands.

He's full of prospectus of Russia.
The future heart.

I nosh over duck at a place I can't afford.
I'm mortified by what I can confess
that has nothing to do with him.

My friends spoon food into their mouths.
With a frisson.

Shouldn't my sleeping with me glow with me? I think so.

Was he with the longbow her father?

the grave mugging
the grave overexposed
my finger blocking the grave
the grave and her mother

She would not suffer.

She's not my mother but a message in an owl's beak. I gave it to
her because she rose in the air and headed for holiday. At the
party at our house someone stopped Mordecai. There was a shoe
print on his face. He left early.

The soldier brake in.

A pack of loose feathers.

Leading up to me. She curtsied. She tingled.

God, beautiful-marksman, says, "If I aim, move."

Between the stalactites, I imitate a hologram.

I have a vampire.

A pack of loose feathers.

Then she rushed out of the pool and, pointing to her slit, asked,
"My lord and my love, what is this?" "Your cunt," said he, and she
replied, "You have no shame," and slapped him. "Your vulva," said
he, and the other sister pinched him shouting, "Bah, that is an
ugly word." "Your womb," said he, and the third sister knocked
him over, saying, "Fie, have some shame."

Don't do this again.

This is a platter of fruit…viz a viz…opulent requests for

                breaks the body.

Without that, there's no point.

I tell him _____ was cruel to me.

He says I want to make you lose control.

I order a burger. I'm like if I have to be here.

He gets a burger too.

I say I see a string of white lights strung on a building close by.

I say   You can't you won't be able to.

And yet I want

they want to finish pretty badly. And I am

very polite.

This is a story about the maverick garden.

We talk in the car. We laugh a little. He is relieved that we laugh.
And so am I.

I want to laugh more.

He says that I am not different.

I say   I see a string of white lights strung on a building close by.

I say   You can't you won't be able to.

I return, therefore, to my theory on dyads. This way of thinking
originated probably in 1995 when I met a boy who made stews
and wore red sweaters. They reached for each other and they felt
so young.

Tale told of a fisherman, many, many fishermen who stole the
rumpled clothes by the shore and returned home with a girl with
a certain damn twist to her lips. She's a selkie, a silky. She's a seal.
She'll never be at home.

I think of holding children though and do sometimes.
After a while (with stewed carrots)
I whap my tail. I really don't care.

I look at my stomach in the bathroom.
I think of myself ten years ago when I first started working.
How I smiled at everyone behind my register.

SONOGRAM

I dreamed my mother collapsed inside of me
and nothing else was true.
I was still and I cupped my heart's stream
into my heart's mouth and
I could do nothing.
This is to say I was a child.
Casting nets of silver so you feel
the feeling of

this is my job: the child is living
and can be named for a dog.
A dog would be pure black emotion.
A terrycloth terror we'll rub on our bodies
and hold onto for fear of

she was a child. She was a child.
And in her child she felt her mother's sadness.
I want to her to feel it
for how can I touch her, the beatitude, the velvet veto.
What hasn't happened yet.
What it feels like to hold onto the stairs for help.

That's every story—medea plumming candle.
Dead-rot dog
finking across the need to know.

As I stand in front of the "victim."
She's garrulous as we practice on the child
on her dovetail joints that despite everything
thrill and thrill and thrill.

This, of course, is a secret.

You call the black horse, "Father."
You are followed all your life.
There is a canyon.
There is a lighted stage.
There is a waiting audience.

Write a poem in three stanzas—described below:

1. Describe the canyon from the stage.
2. Describe the audience from the canyon.
3. Describe the stage from the canyon.
4. Make a horse run through all three stanzas.

UNTITLED

I

Some say I'm a violent person. I just like to get souped up.
I had my hands on a 4x4 once—cantered, hot-damn kinda body.
I could've stayed like that for days. And I did. 78 hours.

The owner didn't come.
The misogynist didn't come.
My late great Chachi, alas, didn't come.

But I was there. Even though the Muse didn't show, I was there.

I made love until they rang the buzzer.

I was a borealis and it was all he could do
to hold me in a diesel cup.
I poured out like rain unto tears.

Standing out in the cranberry park, my champion said,
"I hated it with him and I hated it with you."

II

Some say I'm an emotional person. I think I just like to eat a lot.
I like to say yes on the telephone and go to UPS to pick up my
packages.

One came the other week—too late for Christmas—too early for
the new year. It shammied and shimmied.
A book, he said, of course of my childhood.

Can it mean that you are a Taoist? Featherproof? Holidaypipe?
It was just that she sat so together.
That she gritted her teeth while I looked for handlebags.
She said, "You don't know."

And it was her look of her waiting for me.
A brook so cold—standing in—
looking for the tritri fishes.

III

I'm red. I go fast. I have a leather interior. I have a halogen stereo.
They all wish they could stay in me.

They say:

> Clean me.
> Write me.
> Hold me.

I'm gainin' ground all the time.

Carolina
Dakota
Alabama sans souci.

I have a killer sound track.
I'm in animation making all the difference.

They're in a red room.
Do none of them die?

Shahrazad: The Vizier's daughter.
Meant to be read aloud.
An arachnid of the hysterical sort.
A fiction. A fiction. You know the kind.

Sultan: ....

Shahrazad: Ferny breasts   amplification
recalcitrant talkshow. I can look back.
That grows women,
a fiction. Stay there.

Sultan: Soap on a rope.

Shahrazad: The phone rang last night. Late at night.
Happy smock.
No "some assembly required."

Sultan: I have an army.
Did I tell you I have an army?

Shahrazad: My pretty, pretty, pretty.

Sultan: Who he can. Who he chooses.

Shahrazad: Who she can. Who she chooses.

Given and taken away.
If you really love me. Shytooth.
Fandangled.
If you say to the plush, if you really love me.

It hangs deep in his robes, a delicate clapper at the center of a bell.
Collapsible.
Like a surgical procedure on TV.
We saw it breathe in and out of itself.
A girl buying her first practical car with no tape player.
AM, I love you. FM, I love you.
You fill the tank.
You dunk the girls.
You are a glass house.
You are the glass tigers breathing in and out of themselves.

Gardeners remark on it. In particular, my gardener.
He is known for his Buick of disguises
and for throwing sticks and throwing sticks.
It was terrible and grew mortal and slick.

My warriors have drawn on themselves the symbol of children,
of those who never die.
This is why no one tries to kill them.

We all want to go back to the amniotic source.
The question of being enraptured,
meaning dumbfounded, meaning encased, meaning
that your head does not break the surface.
Every sweet-trellised.

If I pick a candy for you, it is wrong.
If I pick a bicycle for you, it is wrong.
Where will I lay my manger of everything that came before you?
If you love me, you knew me then.

Rapscallion.
Creamy.
Screamy.

If you really love me, live to live it down.
I die so that you are a sliver.
I die so that you are a daughter.

BATGIRL

I don't want to invite those darker envelopes of me waistband
in the bookbible darkness.
I have sentiments and pretty candy and snowmen.

And snowmen who adore me.
and I'm angry
and I leave the concert area quietly in my batgirl pleather.
So everyone looks at me, me, me.

And I apologize because I'm supposed to.
And I rival your friend
who flew with you as you were sad to "new york."
Where mortals drink brandy in my getting-expensive café.

She sits slowly beside me on the train.
And that I love her has no bearing
on the idea that
I feel like the ten thousandth lamb.
I was there when he
when you said—no presents.
Maybe we'd just ask everyone
to bring flowers to the church.
Can you imagine loving someone like that?

Dear Elation, There Is Something Else You Didn't Know

You cannot be two places at once:
wearing earrings for my return
and packing up every mirror in your apartment.

You must not dream for the rest of us.
You must dream for the rest of us.

Whatever you choose. Get into the car and drive.

I often think of our one memory—why is that—
when we have known each other so long?

There was amber light over the high walls of a city.
It is an old city.

Boys and colts were playing soccer in the plaza of the kings.
The bay is reflected of amber, filtered through lantern-lights.

You were my friend.

Flapping hair.
Rife.
Feathering dress.

You cannot watch the same movie at twenty, at twenty-five.

Her blushes mean a different moment.

So, when this holds back
make plans,
make haste.

Make a jagged point in the rock.
You are the rock.

TORO LIBRE

If a bull is very brave and I am unable to kill him, a quiet arises within me and all who are watching. For this bull, I will ask to set him free. He will live out his days at peace, never again to fight in the ring.

—PALOMA DE LOS REYES
Her *Light Journal*

SCENE: THIS IS YOUR COUNTRY

I'm tired only in Technicolor.
Clotted corn. A beast on the ride.

In my life, I genuflect
hatted and star-aware.

1. beast
2. no beast

An audience empathizes.

In captivity, Shahrazad
would bear him three children.

We put on
the show for ourselves.
A modern something.
Me with you with
your tears on your face.

Says no when means shut up. Shut up.
Nanghihinyang.

A cappingsizing streamer on starfish on its tail.
Mythology.

I know you in your life
when you draw water
for my beautiful child.

faith came to me like
my marie in pain

a corpulent debtor
maxes out and throws
galvanizes boondock cards

_____ of hearts

_____ of hearts

my darker lexicon
marie : off

my name is   we know
the other of goodways and
island girls waving
"down there"
handkerchiefs

blink

_____

blink

the difference is important
between
work

we harness the same
horse to both
my ancient and ancient

SCENE: RUFINA DE LOS REYES FAILS TO RETURN

She said, do you know who I am? I'm a doctor.
I'm here to set every bone out of the third-world metatarsal.

We were giddy, utterly serious & with no clue who we were
we picked an 80-point diamond ring.

I am a star, a request

for more lighters.

That vampire in the twelve bottled-up of vampires.
is only one in the assembly line of cawing, fainting vampires.

I'm here to punctuate those rums and silences.

Paloma, Because I Love Her

I am an uproarious cup.

A girl. Pale clear shift. Ludicrous and twinged in the dark.

I have a sympathetic palate.
I can eat anything that doesn't criticize me.

I am short hair and small breasts. I smile at birthday cards.

I lurch from my seat.

I wear lipstick. I sweep up glass.

Heedless.

In all my selves, I am a corroded quilt.
But I welcome all the times.

The googly-eyed world.

Shreds of the self: peculiar, bitten, star-worthy.

In New York, I will drive and play piano.

When I was unfair with her,
I brought her bread and cream cheese.

A fancy cup of orange juice.

The success of the liberation movement left thousands of young

men without a cause, uneducated, unemployed

and accustomed to violence.

One accused. One was.

> Like my *teacher* when will you come?

Confession is unto lukewarm oxen.

(sun-song

> lariated cities)

No, I can't forget this evening.

> When men fall down, do they not get up?

> Gorgeous robe.

OF MY FURY

Children lift tiles from the bathroom. I employ them.
I give one a machete.
I give the other a borrowed life.
Together we cut cane on the Asian-American mollusk.

Of my fury,
I make Cheeto-straight-A's.

Of my fury,
I come like a joint popping into place.

Of my fury,
I give you my shark fin. You make a necklace of it.
I hate you more.

Of my fury,
I buy electronica.

Of my fury,
A cumulo-wind blows into the dear and blasted soldier
wanting to "come clean."

Of my fury,
A grass Moses.

Of my fury,
I feel into them. Stuffing them into Wonder Woman bracelets
and repelling my own bullets.

"Last night," you say, "I woke and the city falls on me."

She was very concerned with the chair.

1 tsp. coriander. 2 leaves mint.

Once, I shipped my sister's broken hand to my mother.

For laughs.

You say, "The soldiers cut off her hair."

My feet don't like this. They don't want to carry anything.

Three of us died in one sense:

Toyang of cholera, Lelai of cholera, Charing of cholera.

"Last night," she says,

"I dreamed of ships in a very foreign tongue.

I was holding the velvet rose as they plowed away."

How to Make Your Daughter an American (Again)

2   Roses (velvet preferred)
2¼   Roses (even softer)
1   Good Dog

You are a dog. Never talk to her, dog.
The Transylvania architects are talking.

If in doubt, build a balcony.

I am not apart from her accoutrements.
I am crystal
and sea-egg.

I am more prone or, rather, more prone *to*.

Tom the architect says—the lamp is ugly
and I have a vampire with spangles in her cape

and Spencer Tracy in her eyes.
She plucks and eats pomegranate seeds
from the busted-up geode.

PALOMA'S LIGHT JOURNAL, JUNE 6TH

What will you do if I am $11.92, a coffer of brilliant hair?
I set my lands in order, behold, I reinvent.

In the kitchen they are looking for coals. "Morning," she says.
To find the ruby of a man set in. The status of a man.
Breeze of a fish. Freeform. Indelicate.

Speak to us of the radiantstone.
Regularly the call of flutes redolent, whip-like.

How do you rise up in the assembly of people
dribbled together for quiescence.
How to interrupt the meter of their foreheads and yours
glinting in the branching glass.

Come back to me, here, under the red pepper lights.

New York (Fairest of 10,000 Remix)

Out among the cattails
Paloma is giving birth.

I'm putting her planks in season,
her well-taken voice and Juliet crystals.

No cars. Go.
A slasher.
A paper that makes him free.

She knows no one but
is introduced to everyone in the City.
She asks for fruit juices.

Build your wolf.
Your kind pelt.
Your kind claw.

Only don't tell me—I'm sleeping.

Asian-American Food Poem

I'm better than them all
she said knitting her eggplant costume.
Though I am in despair, I have internet access.

I've been admitted to the fiesta.
I drank beer, pinched the children,
admired the dogs.

The fact that he's filipino and sings really hard into the mike
makes me lie unprotected with only bangles on.
I'm "one of those."
I mean I'm also filipino.

That's an understatement-underwear.

This is so similar to my accident,
my fuckapoet syndrome: *I have a beautiful*
I inform the others.
It's young yet and full of bile and sylvester.

Cushioning up to what she really wants.

I took my earring out. Had dinner with New York.
Spent the night with New York.

I mean. It helps to see my body, my Orthotricyclen.
Grinning and standing by the cake.

All while I am trying on my butterfly kite.
I've made myself smaller and smaller
so as to be able to sit atop my contraption.
The only thing is I would like to fly this kite as well.
I want to be in both places. Atop and below.
But always engaged in the butterfly.

I want to be your undergraduate girl.
Your girl of golden headbands
and trusting environments.
I'm rare like this. I want to find out what I already know

which is my heart in a basin,
washing the hands with

I look it up all the time. I look up other people's love all the time.
I'm an expert on "falling on new york."

You give and you give you give when you do not want to give
you give you give you give when you do not want to give.

Because I am more than just myself. I am my dreaming self
getting better at this.

I saw the best songs of my magician. A girl, three girls pay this toll out on macaw naval bases. Subic/Clark/Olongapo. These were the splinted wings.

I crawled to the other side of the cage.

This was not safe as the Fabergé recesses of men out on liberty are never safe. Future my grandmothers—feeling soldiers with big cola and a limited view of All You Can Eat. If you can't eat it. Throw it out. My girl hungry. My girl learning the sweet sword. Big arcs of molten.

I mean her country big-bottomed and an embarrassment at the Beauty Pageant of Worthwhile. Who smiled too much and wrote to me every night.

Tomorrow I will not be a maid.

Whose husbands were whacked off at the knee. Holding the brown bell of revolution and the lantern of disgust. One day my land will be mine and will pass through my generations like a last view of the flowering oasis.

Who hated their own supernatural but nevertheless bade me lift up my voice for blistering America. Who tore out their own hair for lack of a less hurtful affection and with these strands spun my traje de luces that I might face the bull of inadequacy with the anger of many generations silenced and friendless and witchless.

Paloma, I'm with you in New York
where you are madder than I am.
I'm with you in New York where I am only a reader.
I'm with you in New York where my readership
beseeches me, buys me the books.
I'm with you in New York where what's yours is mine.

SCENE: YOURS
TIME: YOURS

These are projects of shadowy, camphor parents.
Sometimes we can see them in museums.
I have affixed the anthropological data for you.

I want to make sure that you understand,
that you keep your promise to your reasonable history.
I will not have you whirling around
like a professional candystriper.

And if I am afraid?

You will not be afraid.

Tagalog is the official language of the Republic of the Philippines.

Paloma Loves: "Gayon na lamang ang pag-ibig ng Diyos sa sanlibutan, kaya ibinigay niya ang kanyang bugtong na Anak, upang ang sumampalataya sa kanya ay hindi mapahamak, kundi magkaroon ng buhay na walang hanggan" is Tagalog for John 3:16 in the Bible: "For God so loved the world that He gave His only begotten Son, that whosoever believeth in Him should not perish, but have everlasting life."

Scene: a Loom: "Ito ay isang pagdasal para sa kapatid ko" is Tagalog for "This is a prayer for my sister."

Scene: This Is Your Country: "Nanghihinyang" is a Tagalog verb meaning to wish, to long for, to regret.

Scene: Rufina de los Reyes Fails to Return: In 1941, the Japanese bombed the city of Manila. It was after this bombing that my great-grandmother, Rufina de los Reyes, disappeared from her family.

Passage: This poem is after Allen Ginsberg's "Howl."

Alice James Books has been publishing exclusively poetry since 1973. One of the few presses in the country that is run collectively, the cooperative selects manuscripts for publication through both regional and national annual competitions. New regional authors become active members of the cooperative, participating in the editorial decisions of the press. The press, which historically has placed an emphasis on publishing women poets, was named for Alice James, sister of William and Henry, whose fine journal and gift for writing went unrecognized within her lifetime.

Typeset and Designed by Dede Cummings